Praise for *The Ultimate College Financial Aid Guide*

Wish I'd had this resource years ago!
This is the most helpful book I've ever read on the process of obtaining financial aid. As a life-long learner and student, I appreciate how the author demystifies the process of obtaining college funding. She good-naturedly holds the readers hand while expertly explaining the (previously) terrifying concepts of a "financial aid letter," including those notoriously anxiety-producing elements such as "Pell Grants," "unsubsidized loans," and "institutional aid."

Dr. Barbu expertly demonstrates how to compare colleges and even how to determine future out-of-pocket college-related-costs. By the time you're finished reading this book, you'll understand the financial aid application process start to finish, and you'll be able to identify the colleges that will provide the best academic and financial fit. Whether this book is for yourself or your college-bound teen, you won't find a better financial aid resource. Thank you Dr. Barbu!

- Diane Metcalf, Author, Lemon Moms Series

D0583749

Simplifies the process from start to finish

I've worked in higher Ed for over 10 years and feel that I have a pretty good understanding about the FinAid system, but as I started researching for my own son, I realized there was so much more to learn.

This book simplifies the entire FinAid process from start to finish and I LOVE how it provides examples from various institutional structures. I plan to use everything I've learned to help myself as a mother, but also got some ideas on how to simplify things for my students and their parents as well.

- Alexis

What you need to know about financial aid! I've been at a university for 39 years and learned a lot!

This book is current, thorough, and easy to follow. I was thrilled to even see mention of experiential learning as a consideration. Also, Dr. Diana recommends a rule of thumb for limiting student loans. A pet peeve of mine is spending too much on loans! If I could give six stars l would!

- Dr. Phil Rosenkrantz

THE ULTIMATE COLLEGE FINANCIAL AID GUIDE

Also By Dr. Diana Barbu

The Ultimate College Admissions
Guide:
*Help Your Teen Get In, Go Through, &
Graduate College (almost) Debt Free*

THE ULTIMATE COLLEGE FINANCIAL AID GUIDE

Understand the Aid Offer & Ask For More Money

Diana Barbu, PhD

Copyright © 2021 Diana Barbu, PhD

All rights reserved. No part of this publication may be reproduced, distributed, or transmitted in any form or by any means, including photocopying, recording, or other electronic or mechanical methods without the prior written permission of the publisher, except in the case of brief quotations embodied in reviews and certain other non-commercial uses permitted by copyright law.

While the author has made every effort to provide accurate Internet addresses at the time of publication, the author/publisher does not assume any responsibility for errors or changes that occur after publication.

ISBN-13: 978-1-7361875-1-7 (paper)
ISBN-13: 978-1-7361875-0-0 (e-book)

READ THIS FIRST

I found that readers get more success with this book when using the Excel version of the **College Cost Comparison Spreadsheet**.

Use it to centralize all the values from all your financial aid letters. It will help you:
(1) determine your out-of-pocket costs for each college, and
(2) compare colleges by price.

To download the College Cost Comparison Spreadsheet go to:
- www.collegetalk.us, or
- scan the code below

To my wonderful husband Adrian

Contents

Foreword

by Prof. Maya Ackerman, Ph.D.

When I applied for financial aid, I made a terrible mistake. I had added an extra zero to my father's salary. As a top student with financial need, I qualified for a full ride. Instead, I ended up with a meager $100 in government support. I had no idea that I could appeal my financial aid or how to go about it. I haven't even realized that I had made a mistake, assuming that I did not qualify. This unfortunate error came to light later when, running out of options, I desperately tried to get more financial aid. By then, it was too late to erase that zero.

This unfortunate mistake had undoubtedly made my early adult life harder than it had to be. On the bright side, I had fallen in love with college, where I was destined to spend my entire life - a decade earning my three degrees, two postdoctoral fellowships, and as of today, seven years as a professor. Over the years, I've had the privilege to teach and mentor thousands of young people.

Despite my many years in academia, I found myself reading this book primarily as a parent, mother to a young teenager. It is terrifying to imagine that my only child will leave the nest in a few short years. Helping my son through the college admission process will be one of my most essential acts of parental guidance. His college years will be crucial in shaping the rest of his life, both personally and professionally.

The US college system is composed of remarkably varied options, differing not only on educational criteria but also in the social experiences offered on many gorgeous campuses. This variety gives our children the opportunity to select an education that is just right for their needs. This varied terrain can be difficult to navigate, and financial considerations can make this choice particularly challenging. Knowing how to navigate the complex landscape of college admission and financial aid can make a world of difference.

This is where Dr. Diana Barbu comes in. Her knowledge and profound insight into the educational landscape is unparalleled. Dr. Diana has a Ph.D. in Higher Education and many years of experience in the very institutions that create and coordinate the college experience. She has been instrumental in forming my understanding of the college admission process and financial aid. In this book, Dr. Diana generously shares her knowledge and insight into these complex issues with remarkable clarity.

Dr. Diana demystifies the financial aid letter and shows how to compare letters from vastly different institutions. She discusses the unique role of the first year versus subsequent years and how to balance financial considerations against other essential criteria. One of the most critical parts of the book is how to appeal your financial aid letter, giving you the power to negotiate with colleges in an effective, respectful manner.

Dr. Diana shares little-known mechanisms that can make a massive difference to your family's financial situation as you send your child off to college. It is overwhelming to realize how much more affordable my college experience would have been if the 18-year-old me or my parents had the information offered in this book.

College is a beautiful time. Over the years, I've watched many young people blossom into self-assured, responsible adults ready to take on the challenges of adult life as they walk in their regalia to receive their degree. In a few short years, you will join your child to celebrate one of their greatest achievements, their college graduation.

Prof. Maya Ackerman, PhD.,
Computer Science & Engineering
Santa Clara University
CEO & Co-Founder of WaveAI

Introduction

The college admissions process can be long and involved. It starts innocent enough in high school or maybe even middle school when you and your teen probably began having conversations about college. If you are like my mom, you probably started talking to your child about college as soon as they started walking. I don't remember a time in my life where college did not come up, and she made it abundantly clear that one day I'll go to college. I still remember myself vividly admiring her earrings; I must have been in 6th grade when she promised that they'd be mine the day I get admitted to college. I still have and wear those earrings.

College conversations can be exhilarating and sometimes fun. Surveys show that while parents and teens share similar concerns about college costs and debt, they differ in how far away from home the college should be. Most parents want their teen to attend a college "fewer than 250 miles" from home, while most teens want to attend college "more than 250 miles" from home, and these preferences have remained unchanged since 2006.[1] That being said, scholars found that more than 75% of the students tend to attend college within 50 miles of their homes (Goldrick-Rab 2016, p. 192). Like most teens out there, I wanted to go to college in another city but couldn't, as college costs and debt were a major concern for my family. Therefore, we had to find the best option for quality education at an affordable price. And, similar to the research findings, I ended up attending college in my hometown, and it just so happened that the college was two blocks away from my home. And you know what? I loved it; I loved the college experience, the learning, and the friends. If you have been having some of these conversations, know that you are not alone, and everything will work out just fine.

College is one of the few investments that pay off. College graduates earn about $1 million more than high school graduates over their lifetime and secure better jobs and salaries. They "can spend more money, contribute to the local tax bases, attract business investment, and are more likely to start their own enterprises" (Goldrick-Rab 2016, p. 194). Additionally, college graduates are healthier, more civically engaged, earn more, and are better positioned to invest in their children's education. On the other hand, scholars have found that individuals who cannot attend college are "systematically locked out of nearly every decent-paying job opportunity, every safe neighborhood, and every opportunity to create safe futures for [their] children" (p. 256).

However, educational debt ballooned to $1.6 trillion in 2020, [2] and college costs have gone up during the past several years. A college education today "is more expensive than ever."[3] Because of this being mindful about investing in a college education is very important.

While the benefits of going to college tend to be significant, navigating the college admission process can be intimidating. Here is a list of steps involved in college admission:
1. The college selection
2. The college application
3. The financial aid application
4. The acceptance letters
5. The college aid offer (the financial aid letters)
6. Asking for more aid
7. Finding the best academic and financial fit

8. Committing to or depositing with a college

While each one of these steps looks simple, the reality is that they can be quite involved and include specific actions. At the same time, each step may be equally important in facilitating the transition between high school and college. There are numerous guides out there that cover the first three (3) steps. The mechanics and details associated with the last five (5) steps tend to be more esoteric, requiring specialized expertise and knowledge. Therefore, this book focuses on these critical steps – identifying essential elements involved in choosing a college and explaining what's involved in analyzing the financial aid offers you will receive from each college.

Once you and your teen complete the college and financial aid applications, college admission officers decide who gets in. Teens who get accepted will receive a college acceptance letter. A few weeks/months after receiving the college acceptance letter, your teen will receive a college aid offer. The college aid offer is the financial aid letter (FAL).

Many FALs will show you how much college will cost for the first year and what types of aid (grants, scholarships, loans, and work-study) a college provides from the primary three sources (federal, state, and college) to help the teen cover the college costs. However, they may not provide you with the actual out-of-pocket costs.

The out-of-pocket costs are very important, as these values can inform the college decision. This book shows you how to determine your out-of-pocket costs, understand the categories of aid, compare colleges, ask for more aid, and understand how your aid may change in subsequent years.

By the end of the book, you will:
- Know how to read financial aid letters (FAL) from any college
- Understand each element included in the FAL (total cost of attendance, Pell Grant, unsubsidized loans, institutional aid, etc.)
- Be able to determine your out-of-pocket cost for each college and compare colleges using these values (using the College Cost Comparison Spreadsheet)
- Learn how to ask for more aid
- Understand what happens to your aid in subsequent years
- Determine how much debt it's safe to take on to finance a college education

After reading this book, you'll be able to identify the college that provides the best academic and financial fit for you and your teen.

***

The Ultimate College Financial Aid Guide will help you compare colleges on costs using the financial aid letter FAL. This book points parents and teens to accurate and reliable data sources and includes up to date research findings to inform the college decision process.

The book is structured as follows: the first chapter includes sample FALs from four colleges and intends to showcase these letters' diversity. The second chapter explains each element that might appear in a FAL and the requirements associated with it.

Chapter 3 explains how to understand the four sample FALs, standardize them, and determine the out-of-pocket costs for each college. As you will see, none of the various total amounts provided through the sample FALs are the actual out-of-pocket costs. Additionally, the out-of-pocket costs were higher than the various total included in the FALs. This chapter will help you calculate your out-of-pocket costs and compare colleges.

Chapter 4 shows you how to ask colleges for more merit and need aid. Chapter 5 discusses how the aid may change after the first year. Finally, Chapter 6 provides data points that can help inform your final college selection decision.

The financial aid offers may offset or may actually *increase* the cost of college. The tools in this book will help you reduce your risk and make college more affordable.

CHAPTER 1: Sample Financial Aid Letters

One thing that is quite common and unnerving across higher education and colleges is the lack of standardization. I've been working in higher education for more than a decade, and I lost track of how many times I ran into it. Financial aid is one of these non-standardized areas, and, as a result, FAL can be unique to each college.

In terms of format, some colleges may send their FALs as a booklet or brochure through snail mail. Others may send students emails with directions on how to access the financial aid offer on the college's website.

In terms of elements, the FAL should include information on the cost of attendance, grants and scholarships, loans, work-study, or other employment options. It may also include the total out-of-pocket cost for attending the college for the first year. In reality, some letters may consist of all of these elements, while others may include bits and pieces of this information. Finally, some FALs may be tentative and may only include estimated costs and awards. All in all, each FAL has its look, feel, and readability.

Here are four sample financial aid letters that a student received recently. You'll see from scanning these letters that determining the amount of money that parents and students need to prepare to cover the cost of the first year of college (or the out-of-pocket cost) is not straightforward.

These four sample letters intend to showcase how differently each college organizes its FAL. If you are finding yourself confused after reading through these letters, know that you are not alone. Anyone is likely to struggle with reading them.

As you scan through these letters, don't worry about the meaning of each scholarship, grant, loan, or work-study. We'll discuss each of these elements in Chapter 2, and in Chapter 3, we'll dissect each sample FAL, calculate the out-of-pocket cost for each college, and then compare colleges on out-of-pocket costs.

Table 1: College A - Financial Aid Letter

Cost of Attendance			
	Tuition and Fees	$	15,500
	Room	$	7,000
	Board	$	6,000
	Total Direct Costs	$	28,500
	Estimated Books & Supplies	$	1,350
	Estimated Other Expenses	$	3,700
Total Costs		$	33,550
College A: Gift Aid			
	State Grant	$	5,900
	Federal Pell Grant	$	2,000
	College A Scholarship	$	3,000
	Presidential Scholarship	$	3,000
Total Grants and Scholarships		$	13,900
Total Direct Cost (total direct costs - total grants and scholarships)		$	14,600
Student Loans			
	Subsidized Direct Loan	$	3,500
	Unsubsidized Direct Loan	$	2,000
Total Student Loans		$	5,500
Your Remaining Direct Cost		$	9,100
Additional Resources			
	College Work-study	$	2,000

Table 2: College B - Financial Aid Letter

Estimated Cost of Attendance			
Tuition	$ 47,000		
Fees	$ 780		
Estimated Books & Supplies	$ 1,000		
Housing & Board	$ 15,300		
Other Expenses	$ 2,300		
Transportation Fee	$ 900		
Total Estimated Cost	$ 67,280		

College B Financial Aid Offer	Fall	Spring	Total
Pell Grant	$ 1,000	$ 1,000	$ 2,000
College B Named Scholarship	$ 2,000	$ 2,000	$ 4,000
College B Scholarship	$ 11,500	$ 11,500	$ 23,000
Estimate College B Need Based Grant	$ 750	$ 750	$ 1,500
Federal Direct Subsidized Loan	$ 1,750	$ 1,750	$ 3,500
Federal Direct Unsubsidized Loan	$ 1,000	$ 1,000	$ 2,000
Parent PLUS Loan	$ 14,640	$ 14,640	$ 29,280
Federal Work-study	$ 1,000	$ 1,000	$ 2,000
Total			$ 67,280

Net Cost after All Aid:	$ 0

Table 3: College C - Financial Aid Letter

Estimated Billed Costs		Fall	Spring	Total
	Tuition and Fees	$ 14,400	$ 14,400	$ 28,800
	Room and Board	$ 5,500	$ 5,500	$ 11,000
Total		$ 19,900	$ 19,900	$ 39,800
Other Estimated Non-Billed Costs				
	Books and Supplies	$ 425	$ 425	$ 850
	Personal Expenses	$ 1,000	$ 1,000	$ 2,000
	Transportation Expenses	$ 350	$ 350	$ 700
Total		$ 1,775	$ 1,775	$ 3,550
Estimated Financial Aid Package				
	College C Grant	$ 1,300	$ 1,300	$ 2,600
	Tuition Waiver	$ 3,000	$ 3,000	$ 6,000
Total		$ 4,300	$ 4,300	$ 8,600
Estimated Total Billed Costs				
	Estimated Cost of Attendance	$ 21,675	$ 21,675	$ 43,350
	Annual Financial Aid	$ 4,300	$ 4,300	$ 8,600
Total		$ 17,375	$ 17,375	$ 34,750

Table 4: College D - Financial Aid Letter

Award	Award Total
College D Freshman	$ 2,000
Housing Grant	$ 3,000
College D Award	$ 22,000
College D Award 2	$ 3,000
College D Grant	$ 7,000
Fed. Unsubsidized	$ 2,000
Federal Subsidized Loan	$ 3,500
Total Award	$ 42,500
On-Campus Direct Cost	$ 54,500
Total Financial Aid Award	$ 42,500
Year 1 Total Out-of-Pocket Cost	$ 12,000

You are eligible to earn up to $2,000 in work-study.

CHAPTER 2: Understand the Elements of the Financial Aid Letter

The following section discusses the types of aid that could appear in a typical financial aid letter. This section explains the most common types of grants and scholarships, loans, and campus employment opportunities that may be awarded to students. Additionally, this section details each award, who is eligible for it, and what to do to ensure that the award gets renewed for subsequent years.

It is important to note that some of the funds colleges describe as "financial aid" come with a cost to students or their parents. This is especially the case for loans. Additionally, a financial aid award is not a prize; rather, it describes a source of funds that has been assigned by the college as a means for covering the cost of attendance. All the financial aid awards are included in the FAL.

That being said, depending on your eligibility, a comprehensive FAL may include some or all of the following five elements:

Element 1: Total cost of attendance (for the upcoming academic year)

Element 2: Gift aid – the source and amount of gift aid that doesn't need to be repaid

Element 3: Net price or out-of-pocket cost – the net price and how much the student will have to pay for one year of college after gift aid (grants and scholarships) has been subtracted from the total cost of attendance

Element 4: Loan aid – the source and amount of loans. These will need to be repaid with interest

Element 5: Earned aid – the source and amount of aid earned by the student through work-study or campus employment

Financial Aid Letters may not include some of these five (5) elements. For missing elements — especially those that affect the cost of attendance — I will point you to the right source and explain how to look up the data.

Additionally, FALs may not include Element 3 – net price/out-of-pocket costs. Many financial aid letters might include something similar to it, but it may be calculated differently and provided under a different name. For example, while our sample letters (tables 1-4) included various *costs* or *totals,* none of them included the actual out-of-pocket cost. Plus, the *costs* or *totals* provided by our sample FALs are all lower than the actual out-of-pocket cost.

Now let's focus on each of the five elements.

Element 1: Total Cost of Attendance

The first element that should be included in the financial aid letter (FAL) is the total cost of attendance. The cost of attendance is how much it will cost to attend college for one year. The total cost of attendance is also sometimes referred to as "sticker price."

The cost of attendance comprises two sections: (a) direct costs and (b) indirect costs.
Direct costs are paid directly to the college and include:
- Tuition and fees
- Room and board

Indirect costs are costs that students need to **plan** for and are not paid directly to the college. Indirect costs include:

- Books and supplies
- Transportation and other fees

Direct costs need to be paid each semester to register and attend classes, while the indirect costs ensure that everything necessary for college is covered (books, transportation, etc.). It may be tempting to dismiss indirect costs as optional, but scholars found that ignoring them can pose significant challenges to college attendance and success (Goldrick-Rab 2016, p. 235). Students and parents can get a clear idea about out-of-pocket costs at different colleges only when considering both the direct and indirect costs.

Some institutions don't include the total cost of attendance and its components in the FAL. Letters may include only tuition and fees and leave out room and board, while others sum them all up under direct costs. This may happen for various reasons. First off, the cost of attendance is often subject to change, and it can be a hassle for the school to update the financial aid letters' documentation each time it does. Second, some colleges don't finalize the costs of attendance until the spring semester or even late May. If that is the case with your colleges, the cost of attendance figures included in the letter may be estimates or left out altogether.

On the other hand, the exclusion of indirect costs from the financial aid letter can be frustrating. Making sense of the FAL and comparing colleges on costs can be daunting when some of the information is missing. The next section shows you how to access the cost of attendance information that may be estimated or left out of the FAL.

Looking Up the Total Cost of Attendance
There are two ways to get accurate, reliable cost of attendance information: (1) the college's website and (2) College Navigator.

The College's Website
Some financial aid letters may provide a link to a specific location on their website where you can access the direct and indirect costs. Some colleges do a great job providing this information in a way that is easy to read and understand. Others may list information such as tuition and fees by credit hour and list multiple room and board options. This may be the case, especially when the college has various dorms or board/food plans with different pricing structures. These options may make it challenging to predict actual costs when there are so many factors involved. If the cost of

attendance is still difficult to determine using the college's website, try the next option.

<u>College Navigator</u>
The other way to find a college's cost of attendance is through the College Navigator. The College Navigator website is maintained by the federal government and uses data reported by colleges annually.

The College Navigator includes the total cost of attendance. Keep in mind that this information is from the previous academic year. The costs may have changed since the last year, and the new cost of attendance may be slightly higher than what shows up in College Navigator. Tuition, fees, room, board, or any cost component is subject to change over time.

Here's how to access a college's cost of attendance using College Navigator:
- Go to:
  https://nces.ed.gov/collegenavigator/
- Search by college name
- Go to the "Tuition, Fees, and Estimated Student Expenses" section

The values provided through College Navigator may be slightly outdated. It is quite common for a college to increase tuition or other costs if it hasn't done so in a while. College

Navigator will help you find out if your college changed costs during the last few years; if it hasn't, it may do so in the upcoming academic year. While the timing and the exact amount of an increase are hard to predict, typical increases tend to start around 2%. Sometimes these increases impact one or more categories of the total cost of attendance – tuition, fees, room, board, books, etc. Colleges will report these changes to the federal government, but the data reporting process has delays. Hence the "Tuition, Fees, and Estimated Student Expenses" may be higher for the upcoming year than those already listed in College Navigator.

The nice thing about getting the cost of attendance from the College Navigator is the way the information is presented. The living arrangements and "other expenses" are neatly placed into three categories: on-campus, off-campus with family, and off-campus without family. This leads me to the next point.

Living on Campus Requirements
Now it's a good time to talk about the living on-campus requirement. When we seek to determine whether a college is a financial fit, we need to pay attention to the living on-campus requirement.

Many universities — especially the ones geared towards providing a residential experience — have living on-campus requirements. This means that the college requires all freshmen or sophomores (or both) to live on campus.

Living on campus requirements are typically established in response to research findings. There is plenty of student success research out there that points out that students living on campus, especially during the first year or couple of years in college, tend to be more successful. Successful meaning, a smoother transition between high schools and college, getting good grades, proximity to classes, library, advisers, and faculty members, developing good study habits and lasting friendships, returning to college the following semesters and years, and increasing the likelihood for graduation.

Some exclusions apply, and students who live within a certain distance from the university may be exempt from this requirement. Double-check the college's website to determine if the college has such a requirement.

Again, not all colleges have this requirement, but it helps to be aware of it as you assess direct costs.

Element 2: Gift Aid

Gift aid refers to the funds listed as scholarships and grants. Most, if not all, FALs include some grants or scholarships. A comprehensive FAL should include these scholarships and grants grouped under one category that might be referred to as "gift aid."

Funds offered through scholarships and grants do not need to be repaid. The most comprehensive FALs may also separate gift aid by source (i.e., state, federal, college).

Here is a comprehensive list of the types of grants and scholarships that might appear in a FAL. Depending on a student's eligibility, award letters may include some or all of the following:

a) Federal gift aid (grants)
b) State gift aid (grants or scholarships)
c) Institutional gift aid (grants or scholarships)
d) Tuition waivers
e) Athletic scholarships
f) Gift aid from external sources

The following section discusses all these types of gift aid and their specifications.

a) Federal Grants:

Federal grants are provided by the federal government to students and processed by the college. Only students who file the Free Application for Federal Student Aid (FAFSA) are eligible for federal aid. Additionally, the college needs to hold institutional accreditation. Not everyone is eligible for federal funds, and not all colleges are eligible to receive these funds.

To determine if a college is accredited, go to College Navigator and enter the college's name. In the new window, click on the Accreditation section and look at the Institutional Accreditation. Students attending colleges that do not hold institutional accreditation cannot access funds from the federal government. These funds, commonly referred to as Title IV funds, include federal grants (such as Pell Grant and FSEOG), federal loans, and federal work-study. The next section explains each type of federal and Title IV funds.

The Pell Grant
The federal government awards the Pell Grant based on the student's demonstrated financial need. A student can receive up to around $6,500 per academic year. The amount of Pell Grant funds awarded depends on the Student Aid

Index (SAI), formerly known as the Estimated Family Contribution (EFC).

The Student Aid Index (SAI), formerly the Estimated Family Contribution (EFC)
Effective October 1, 2022 the SAI replaces the EFC. In other words, anyone filing the FASFA on or after this date will receive an SAI value rather than an EFC value.

The SAI is an index value "calculated according to a formula established by law," using the information submitted through FAFSA. The SAI does not vary by college; it is "an index that reflects an evaluation of a student's approximate financial resources to contribute toward the student's postsecondary education for the academic year." The EFC was "defined as a measure of how much the student and his or her family can be expected to contribute to the cost of the student's education for the year."[4]

All in all, the federal government calculates the SAI using FAFSA information. Therefore, depending on the SAI value some students receive the full Pell grant amount while others may receive only a fraction of it.

***

It is important to remember that:

- Students and parents (of dependent students) need to re-file the FAFSA every year while students attend college
- The eligibility for the Pell Grant and the amount that a student receives is determined annually
- Retaining the Pell Grant is dependent on the family's finances as well as students meeting "Satisfactory Academic Progress" (SAP) criteria

The "Satisfactory Academic Progress" (SAP) criteria are rules established by each college that measures a student's completion of coursework for them to maintain eligibility for grants and scholarships. For example, some colleges have set the minimum requirement for their SAP standards to be a "C" average for the student's cumulative GPA and expect students not to drop too many classes. Some colleges use one set of SAP criteria for all grants and scholarships, while others have different criteria for each grant or scholarship.

All in all, each college establishes its SAP criteria. The best way to learn about these criteria is to visit the college's website or contact the financial aid office.

Any changes to the parents' income (for dependent students) or personal income (for independent students) will lead to changes in the Pell Grant amount. To access more information on the Pell grant, please visit: https://studentaid.gov/understand-aid/types/grants/pell

The Federal Supplemental Educational Opportunity Grant (FSEOG)

The federal government awards the FSEOG based on demonstrated exceptional financial need. Students who receive the Pell Grant may also be eligible for the FSEOG award. The maximum amount has been around $4,000. The determination for FSEOG eligibility is made by each college based on fund availability. To access more information on the FSEOG please visit: https://studentaid.gov/understand-aid/types/grants/fseog

Federal grants such as the Pell Grant and the FSEOG are gift aid that doesn't need to be repaid.

b) State Aid (Grants or Scholarships)

Typically, these are funds provided by the state to help students cover a portion of college's entire cost. These funds tend to be available for state residents but some states allow non-residents to use them under certain conditions.

State aid — typically scholarships — is merit-based and focused on preventing "brain drain" or attracting academically talented students to the state. Other state aid — typically grants — is geared towards providing college access and awarded to students with demonstrated financial need. Some states offer both grants and scholarships, while others offer only one type of aid.

The best way to learn about these scholarships is to visit the state's website or the college's financial aid office website.

Some states require students to apply for state funds through a specific application separate from FAFSA. State applications may also have their deadlines. Additionally, state aid requirements may change over time; check the state and college website(s) periodically to stay up to date.

State awards follow the same trend as any other type of aid. Specifically, there are SAP criteria established by the state and monitored by financial aid offices. Students who fail to meet these criteria can lose these awards and figure out how to make up the difference in subsequent years. We will discuss award renewability in the next section.

c) College or Institutional Aid

College-specific scholarships or grants are funds that the college or university offers to students for demonstrated financial need (grants) or academic achievement (scholarships), or both. These funds are awarded from the college's reserves or philanthropic funds; hence, they are commonly referred to as *institutional aid*.

These scholarships and grants are usually the largest amounts of gift aid that appear in financial aid letters.[5] In other words, the largest amount of scholarships and grants that a student may receive will typically come from the institution in the form of institutional aid.

These scholarships will typically include the college's name or may sometimes be called presidential scholarships/grants. For example, the financial aid letters for Colleges A, B, and D (Tables 1, 2, and 4) include institutional aid funds that range from $6K to $35K. While their names vary widely, the source of the funds is the same (the college).

It is important to note that students need to apply as early as possible to maximize the amount of funds they can receive.

Each admission and financial aid director interviewed for this book emphasized that institutional funds are limited. Colleges tend to allocate these funds on a first-come-first-served basis — provided that eligibility criteria are met — so the sooner a student applies, the better their chances of receiving them.

For example, let's say that a college has rolling admissions, and students A & B have exactly the same characteristics, GPAs, test scores, and financial standing. Let's say that student A applied in the fall of their senior year, and Student B applied in the spring of their senior year. Student A is more likely to receive institutional aid funds just because of the availability of funds and first-come-first-served determination. By the time Student B applies, these funds may already be depleted; thus, Student B will not get them even though they had the same characteristics as Student A. The date that the application is received matters at certain colleges.

***

If you have been offered institutional aid awards:

- Learn the reason for getting the award
- Learn the renewability criteria

Learn the reason for getting the award
Financial aid letters may include a combination of need and merit aid awards. If it's not immediately apparent, determine whether the awards (scholarship or grants) are need or merit-based.

If an award is need-based, check with the financial aid office to determine if it is tied to the Pell Grant. In other words, are you receiving an award because you are receiving the Pell Grant? If so, keep that in mind because if you lose eligibility for the Pell Grant, you'll also lose this award in the future, your out-of-pocket costs will go up.

Learn the renewability criteria
Once you and your teen have figured out the type of award they received (need or merit), it is essential to understand its renewability criteria. Specifically, it would help if you learned what to do to ensure that your teen keeps receiving it each year. Some awards are only for the first year, while others are renewable for the duration of the studies.

If your award is only for the first year (i.e., non-renewable), your college costs will go up the second year, so plan to have additional funds available to cover these costs starting with the second year.

Some colleges do a great job of explaining the renewability of the awards in the FAL. If the FAL doesn't specify this information, visit the college's website, or contact the financial aid office to learn about the renewability requirements for maintaining these awards all four years.

Institutional aid funds can include substantial amounts of money that could decrease the cost of college or the "sticker price" significantly. It is best to become familiar with and keep track of the renewability criteria for each award provided in the FAL.

d) Tuition Waivers

Some FALs may include tuition waivers. A tuition waiver is a cost that the college is waiving for you. If you get a tuition waiver of $1,000 per semester, this means that you don't have to pay those funds to the college. College C (Table 3) included a $6,000 tuition waiver in its FAL.

Similar to the scholarships discussed above, it is important to learn about how to retain and renew these tuition waivers; otherwise, if you lose the tuition waiver, you'll have to make up the difference, and the out-of-pocket costs will go up.

Some colleges encourage their employees to continue their education while working by providing them with tuition waivers. These programs differ by college; colleges can offer either a discount or a full ride for their employees and sometimes their family members (spouse and children). Each college decides the type of educational benefit for its employees. If you are working at a college or university, contact the HR office to learn more about these benefits.

While tuition waivers tend to be more common for college employees, I've also seen freshmen students not affiliated with the college receive them.

e) Athletic Scholarships

These are awards for athletes. In some cases, the amounts included in these awards can be substantial. These scholarships tend to be renewable, but their renewal may depend on factors outside of your control, such as a coach deciding not to renew a scholarship under certain circumstances or a turnover in coaches, which may lead to non-renewal of the scholarship for athletes recruited by a prior coach. A student-athlete may even lose a scholarship due to injury.

These scholarships may cover a considerable portion of tuition, so be especially mindful of their renewal requirements. Failure to renew can lead to a significant increase in college costs in subsequent years.

f) Gifts From External Sources

These funds are typically scholarships from sources outside of the state, college, or federal government. These generally are the scholarships that are awarded by various entities. A private or local organization may award scholarships for students meeting specific criteria. These are the private scholarships that many students hope for but that few get.

Some of these scholarships are given directly to students in the form of checks to pay general college costs. Other scholarships are awarded to students indirectly through the college. The college then needs to ensure that specific standards are met for the student to continue to receive the funds.

It's great when students can secure these scholarships. Just keep in mind that each college deals with these scholarships differently. Colleges may add them to the existing financial aid packet as soon as you notify the college that you've received it. Under this scenario, the college adds the scholarship to other scholarships and grants that the student may have received, hence decreasing the net price or out-of-pocket costs.

Other colleges may decide to adjust the financial aid packet so that, in some cases, the institutional aid effort is less. In essence, the college would count this scholarship towards a student's financial aid packet and decrease the amount of aid awarded from institutional grants and scholarships; therefore, the net price or out-of-pocket cost would remain the same, but the institutional aid effort would decrease.

Again, each college handles these external scholarships differently. Colleges may provide this information on their websites.

Element 3: Net Price or Out-of-Pocket Cost

The net price is the total cost of attendance minus gift aid (scholarships and grants).[6] Please note that the net price does not include any loans or earned aid in its calculation.

Net Price or Out-of-Pocket Cost

=

Total Cost of Attendance – Gift Aid

The net price is the amount that really matters to parents and students. This value represents how much money a student will have to pay out-of-pocket to attend college for one year. This amount can be covered using family savings, loans, work-study, or other financial options.

It is important to emphasize that the FAL's purpose is not necessary to provide the net price or out-of-pocket costs to parents and students. The FAL shows how much college will cost for the first year and what types of aid (grants, scholarships, loans, and work-study) a college provides from the primary three sources (federal, state, and college) to help the student cover the college costs. Therefore, to determine the net price, parents and students may need to run the net price calculation themselves.

Element 4: Loan Aid

College is expensive, no doubt about that. Decreased state support and erosion of federal funds contributed to increases in college costs and led students and parents to shoulder a larger share of the college costs over time.

One common way of financing a college education is loans. Using loans to pay for college is an investment. I will not bore you with all the statistics, like how college debt has reached $1.6 trillion in 2020, or about how much the college costs have increased over the last several decades[7]—we read about these things every day.

I will say this, however: a college education is an investment that, more often than not, pays good dividends over time. These dividends include a return on investment of over $1,000,000 across the span of a lifetime, competitive advantage in the labor market, and the ability to secure a better paying job.[8] Additionally, individuals who don't attend college are "systematically locked out of nearly every decent paying job opportunity, every safe neighborhood, and every opportunity to create safe futures for their children" (Goldrick-Rab 2016, p. 238). While there are many other investments that we make throughout our lives, few of them may have a return on investment as high as a college education.

A Forbes article from 2014 compared taking on debt to finance a college education to taking on debt to buy a car. Compared to a college education, a car loses value every day. In 2018 the average car price and its subsequent payments were higher than the average student debt and its payments. Specifically, in 2018 the average car loan was $31,000 with an average monthly payment between $381 and $530.[9,10] That same year, a college graduate's average debt was $29,200 with an average monthly payment between $200 and $299.[11,12]

The decision to invest in a college education produces a wide range of benefits. That being said, deciding which college to attend before seeing the price tag may be difficult. Hence the need to understand the FAL and learn how to determine the net price or out-of-pocket costs.

Nowadays, loans are an integral part of the financial aid letter. Financial Aid Letters may include loans if your net price is greater than zero and if you are eligible to receive them. The FAL has only federal loans; however, students may also take out private loans to finance their college education.

It is important to know that while the FAL includes loans, they can be reduced or declined. Some colleges explain in the FAL that you may accept or decline the loans offered. Other colleges accept the loans for you, and you'll need to notify the college if you want to reduce or decline them. Most FALs include steps on how to go about accepting or declining a loan.

If you plan on financing parts of your college education with loans, be mindful of origination fees, interest rates, repayment start dates, and academic requirements to maintain eligibility for them in the future. Additionally, try to borrow as little as possible and always keep track of both the monthly payment and the repayment period.

There are two main ways to secure loans:
   A. The federal government (federal loans)
   B. Private lenders (private loans)

A. Federal Loans
Federal loans can appear in the FAL and are the one of the most common ways for students to finance their education. The amount your teen

may be eligible to receive varies based on the Student Aid Index (SAI) formerly known as the Estimated Family Contribution (EFC), year in college, cost of attendance, and enrollment status.

Each college uses the SAI value for financial aid calculations. While the SAI value remains the same across colleges, the financial aid amount varies as each college has a different cost of attendance.

There are three types of federal loans:
- Direct subsidized loans
- Direct unsubsidized loans
- Parent PLUS loans

Direct Subsidized Loan or *Subsidized Stafford Loan*
This loan is available to students who complete the FAFSA and demonstrate financial need. The government subsidizes this loan by paying the interest rate while a student attends college at least part-time and six months afterward. Dependent students eligible for the loan can borrow up to $3,500 for year 1, $4,500 for year 2, and $5,500 for year 3 and subsequent years. The amounts are slightly higher for independent students. The origination fee for the loan has been around 1.059%, with an interest rate around 2.75%.

Direct Unsubsidized Loan or *Unsubsidized Stafford Loan*

This loan is available to all students who file the FAFSA. Students don't have to demonstrate financial need to be eligible for it. Unsubsidized loans start accruing interest upon disbursement.

A dependent student can borrow up to $5,500 for year 1, $6,500 for year 2, and $7,500 for year 3 and subsequent years. The interest rate has been around 2.75%, with an origination fee around 1.057%.[13]

***

Federal loans are capped. Dependent students eligible for subsidized and unsubsidized loans can only borrow up to a certain amount each year. The amount is capped at $5,500 for year 1 with a maximum of $3,500 in subsidized loans; $6,500 for year 2 with a maximum of $4,500 in subsidized loans; and $7,500 with a maximum of $5,500 in subsidized loans for year 3 and beyond. The amounts are higher for independent students.

These federal loans have different names depending on which school's financial aid letter you read. One study that examined several hundreds of financial aid letters found 136 unique names for unsubsidized loans, and 24 of these names did not even include the word "loan." Some of the names that did not have "loan" in the name included: "Direct Unsub," "Direct Unsub Stafford," and "Fed Direct Unsub Stafford S/S1".[14] Pay close attention to the financial aid letter, and you'll be able to differentiate between grants/scholarships and loans.

Federal Parent PLUS Loans.

Colleges may list Parent PLUS loans in the FAL. For example, College B (Table 2) includes a Parent PLUS loan of $29,280. The Parent PLUS loan is provided by the federal government but is unique in that parents are the ones who apply for it and have the sole responsibility of repaying it. Furthermore, Parent PLUS loans cannot be transferred to the student at any point in time.

If a Parent PLUS loan is right for you, contact the college for guidance on what documentation is needed to start the application. The application steps may differ by college. The federal government has set up comprehensive websites to help parents understand the application process and the implications associated with taking out this loan.

The interest rates are around 6.28%, fixed for the loan's life with a fee around 4.228%[15]. Parents can borrow up to the amount listed in the total cost of attendance minus gift aid, annually. Interest will start accumulating on the loan, and parents need to start making payments on this loan as soon as it is disbursed. Ensure you fully understand this loan's terms and conditions before deciding if it's right for you. To learn more about Parent PLUS loans go to: https://studentaid.gov/understand-aid/types/loans/plus/parent

***

The only way to get access to federal funds is by filing the FAFSA. If you did not file the FAFSA yet, do yourself a favor and file it. Even if you feel that you may not qualify for any aid, file it anyway because many colleges use it to determine the amount of aid a student can receive from the state and the college as well, not just the federal government.

The amounts, interest rates, and origination fees for federal loans may change slightly from year to year. For the latest information, go to the federal student aid website (https://studentaid.gov/understand-aid/types/loans/interest-rates) or the SallieMae website (https://www.salliemae.com/blog/learn-about-stafford-loans/).

B. Private Loans

Private loans are a common way to finance a college education. Private loans don't show up on the financial aid letter because they are not processed through the college's financial aid office. Make sure you have a thorough understanding of the terms of these loans. The origination fees, interest rates, repayment options, and borrower protections may not be as good for private loans as for federal loans. A 2019 study found that private loans "provide fewer consumer protections and repayment options and are typically more costly than federal loans." [16]

***

The consensus is that if loans are needed, it is better to choose a subsidized loan over an unsubsidized loan.[17] In a situation where more funds are needed, it is better to accept the subsidized and unsubsidized loans before committing to the Parent PLUS loan and—if possible—exhaust all federal loan options before considering private loans. The conditions for federal loans tend to be better than the ones for private loans. [18]

Element 5: Earned Aid

Some financial aid letters include earned aid. There are two common ways to earn money while in college: federal work-study and campus employment. If either one of these appears in your FAL, it means that you are eligible to pursue this option. Not all colleges participate in work-study programs or offer campus employment.

Earned aid is contingent upon the student's ability to find a job on campus. While a job is not guaranteed for students eligible for these funds, finding a job on campus is not that difficult. Many colleges hold job fairs specifically for the students who qualify for work-study.

One notable difference between earned funds and other aid types is that the student will have to work to earn a paycheck. Students in these programs will receive a salary just like any other employee at the college on a biweekly or monthly basis. The student can then use the amount earned to assist in covering a portion of the college costs. Students are typically required to work up to fifteen hours per week to earn the amount listed in the FAL.

If your college participates and you are eligible for earned aid, make sure that you accept it as soon as possible. Funds for earned aid are limited and typically awarded on a first come-first-served-basis if other criteria are not specified. Below are more details about the two types of earned aid: federal work-study and campus employment.

Federal Work-study
The federal government provides these funds to students who demonstrate financial need. The average amount of work-study tends to be around $2,000 annually, but the actual amount depends on the college. If you have work-study in your FAL, make sure you accept it as soon as possible as these funds are limited and tend to run out fast. However, not all colleges participate in this program.

Federal work-study is renewable. To renew it, students need to file the FAFSA and meet the eligibility requirements every year. Again, as this is a need-based program, household finances can impact eligibility for these funds.

Campus Employment or Campus Work-study
Campus employment works similarly to federal work-study; however, students may not need to demonstrate financial need to be eligible for it. The college is typically the source of these

funds. Similar to work-study, campus employment funds are limited.

Campus employment may be renewable, but the conditions depend on the college. If you have campus employment included in your FAL, make sure you understand the requirements for renewing the award after the first year.

***

Now you have a clear idea of potential elements of a FAL. Please take a look at your FALs and see how many of these elements they include. Next, we will discuss how to centralize information from all the FALs and determine how colleges compare on net price.

CHAPTER 3: Compare Colleges using Information from Financial Aid Letters

So, here we are! Now that we learned the meaning of each element included in the FAL, it is time to put everything together. This chapter will show you how to make sense of the sample FALs, standardize the information, determine the out-of-pocket costs, and compare colleges.

Remember, the purpose of a FAL is to provide parents and students with information regarding the amount and sources of awards. Financial Aid Letters show how much aid (grants, scholarships, loans, and work-study) is provided from the primary three sources (federal, state, and college). However, parents' and students' purpose is to determine how much each college will cost (the net price or out-of-pocket costs) and how colleges compare to each other. While some FALs provide the out-of-pocket costs, many do not. To make an informed decision, parents and future students need to take an extra step and calculate their out-of-pocket cost using the FAL information.

Before we focus on how to use the FAL information to compare colleges, let's briefly discuss the federal government's FAL standardization efforts.

Financial Aid Letter Standardization

As we've seen before, the diversity of FALs and their terms can be significant. Reading, understanding, and fully interpreting these letters has been challenging even for higher education professionals. This fact has not escaped scholars—or even the federal government.[19,20]

Therefore, the federal government and the National Association of Student Financial Aid Administrators recognized the need for standardization and worked together to develop a standardized template for FALs. A few years ago, the federal government provided the "College Financing Plan" in response.

The College Financing Plan provides a standardized FAL template that helps with reading, understanding, and interpreting the financial aid packet.[21] Also, the template makes net cost or out-of-pocket cost comparisons possible across colleges. While the new template is available, its use has not been mandated. Therefore, although some colleges use it, many don't.

I took this financial aid letter template a step further and developed the *College Cost Comparison Spreadsheet (the Spreadsheet)*. Its goal is to help you centralize all the information included in all the FALs in one place, determine your out-of-pocket costs and compare costs across colleges. It will assist you in making the best possible decision related to selecting and committing to a college.

The Spreadsheet is included in Appendix A, where you will find guidance on how to build it by yourself in Excel. If the last thing you want to do is set up an Excel file with formulas, scan the QR code included below to download the Excel version of *the Spreadsheet*.

As you progress through this chapter, plug in the values from each FAL into this Excel file. Your out-of-pocket costs for each college will automatically calculate, and you'll be able to compare colleges on costs instantly.

Calculating the Out-of-pocket Costs for the Sample FALs

Now we are ready to determine the out-of-pocket costs for each sample FAL and compare colleges. This section explains how to calculate the out-of-pocket cost for each college. The next section shows you how the sample FALs' values were standardized and added to *the Spreadsheet* to allow for cost comparisons.

Table 1 includes the FAL for College A. This letter does a good job explaining the costs associated with attending the college for the first year. The letter details the direct (tuition, housing, food) and indirect costs (books, supplies, and other charges). It describes the awards the student is eligible for, such as gift aid (grants and scholarships), loans, and earned aid (work-study). However, the letter does not provide an actual net price for year 1; it only provides the total direct cost for year 1: $14,600. The indirect costs are left out of the calculation, even though they tend to be quite significant -

$5,050. As discussed before, students and families should always plan for direct and indirect costs — even if the FAL doesn't include all the information.

Table 1: College A - Financial Aid Letter

Cost of Attendance			
	Tuition and Fees	$	15,500
	Room	$	7,000
	Board	$	6,000
	Total Direct Costs	$	28,500
	Estimated Books & Supplies	$	1,350
	Estimated Other Expenses	$	3,700
Total Costs		$	33,550
College A: Gift Aid			
	State Grant	$	5,900
	Federal Pell Grant	$	2,000
	College A Scholarship	$	3,000
	Presidential Scholarship	$	3,000
Total Grants and Scholarships		$	13,900
Total Direct Cost (total direct costs - total grants and scholarships)		$	14,600
Student Loans			
	Subsidized Direct Loan	$	3,500
	Unsubsidized Direct Loan	$	2,000
Total Student Loans		$	5,500
Your Remaining Direct Cost		$	9,100
Additional Resources			
	College Work-study	$	2,000

The out-of-pocket cost or the amount of money that a student would need to prepare to cover

College A's price for the first year is **$19,650**. Here is the calculation for how I got this number:

- The total cost of attendance is $33,550 (direct + indirect costs)
- The total amount of gift aid is $13,900
- The actual net price that a student and the family will need to pay is: $19,650 (total cost of attendance – gift aid)

The rest of the letter elements are contingent on the student taking out loans ($5,500) and finding a job (to earn the funds offered through work-study). As mentioned before, students who are eligible for work-study funds need to find a job on campus and earn those funds. Being eligible for work-study funds does not guarantee the student a job.

Table 2 includes the second sample letter. Reading and understanding this letter can be tricky. Don't get hung up on the $0. Ignore it completely. At first glance, this letter may trick you into thinking that your teen got a full ride. That cannot be further from the truth.

Let's break it down. On the one hand, the letter does a good job explaining the estimated cost of attendance: $67,280. On the other, it fails to differentiate between gift aid (scholarships and grants), loan aid (loans that need to be repaid with interest), and earned aid (work-study). The amount of gift aid is $30,500, loan aid is $34,780, and earned aid is $2,000.

Table 2: College B - Financial Aid Letter

Estimated Cost of Attendance		
Tuition	$ 47,000	
Fees	$ 780	
Estimated Books & Supplies	$ 1,000	
Housing & Board	$ 15,300	
Other Expenses	$ 2,300	
Transportation Fee	$ 900	
Total Estimated Cost	$ 67,280	

College B Financial Aid Offer	Fall	Spring	Total
Pell Grant	$ 1,000	$ 1,000	$ 2,000
College B Named Scholarship	$ 2,000	$ 2,000	$ 4,000
College B Scholarship	$ 11,500	$ 11,500	$ 23,000
Estimate College B Need Based Grant	$ 750	$ 750	$ 1,500
Federal Direct Subsidized Loan	$ 1,750	$ 1,750	$ 3,500
Federal Direct Unsubsidized Loan	$ 1,000	$ 1,000	$ 2,000
Parent PLUS Loan	$ 14,640	$ 14,640	$ 29,280
Federal Work-study	$ 1,000	$ 1,000	$ 2,000
Total			$ 67,280

Net Cost after All Aid:	$ 0

Consequently, the net price/out-of-pocket cost for attending College B for the first year is **$36,780**.

- The total cost of attendance is $67,280 (direct + indirect costs)
- The total amount of gift aid is $30,500
- The actual Net Price that a student and their family will need to pay is: $36,780 (total cost of attendance – gift aid)

Here is the third sample financial aid letter – Table 3. The FAL for College C does a good job providing students and their families with the value that could be interpreted as the net price ($34,750); however, the letter does not list any federal grant/scholarship or loan options. These financial aid letters are for the same student, so the family income information has not changed. It is unclear why the federal options are not listed. Is it that the college does not participate in the federal financial aid program?

Since this student is eligible for the Pell Grant at College A and B, they should be eligible for the same grant at College C. Once the Pell Grant is added to the FAL, the net price for College C is likely to decrease. If the student is interested in this college, they should reach out to the financial aid office to inquire about the federal grant and loan options.

Table 3: College C - Financial Aid Letter

Estimated Billed Costs		Fall	Spring	Total
	Tuition and Fees	$ 14,400	$ 14,400	$ 28,800
	Room and Board	$ 5,500	$ 5,500	$ 11,000
Total		$ 19,900	$ 19,900	$ 39,800
Other Estimated Non-Billed Costs				
	Books and Supplies	$ 425	$ 425	$ 850
	Personal Expenses	$ 1,000	$ 1,000	$ 2,000
	Transportation Expenses	$ 350	$ 350	$ 700
Total		$ 1,775	$ 1,775	$ 3,550
Estimated Financial Aid Package				
	College C Grant	$ 1,300	$ 1,300	$ 2,600
	Tuition Waiver	$ 3,000	$ 3,000	$ 6,000
Total		$ 4,300	$ 4,300	$ 8,600
Estimated Total Billed Costs				
	Estimated Cost of Attendance	$ 21,675	$ 21,675	$ 43,350
	Annual Financial Aid	$ 4,300	$ 4,300	$ 8,600
Total		$ 17,375	$ 17,375	$ 34,750

Without any federal financial aid options, the net price for attending College C for the first year is **$34,750**.

- The total cost of attendance is: $43,350 (direct/billed + indirect/non-billed costs)
- The total amount of gift aid is $8,600

- The actual net price that a student and their family will need to pay is: $34,750 (total cost of attendance – gift aid)

The FAL for College D included in Table 4 may be the hardest to read and understand. First, the total cost of attendance is missing, and it is not clear what is included in the "on-campus direct cost" ($54,500). Second, the letter displays all the awards—loans, grants, and scholarships—in the same section.

Notice that the first loan (Fed. Unsubsidized) does not include the word "loan." As you probably remember, not using the appropriate words to identify loans is not that uncommon.

Reading the FAL for College D poses specific challenges. It is hard to determine the net price for College D for the first year as the total cost of attendance included only the direct costs ($54,000) and failed to include the indirect cost.

Table 4: College D - Financial Aid Letter

Award	Award Total
College D Freshman	$ 2,000
Housing Grant	$ 3,000
College D Award	$ 22,000
College D Award 2	$ 3,000
College D Grant	$ 7,000
Fed. Unsubsidized	$ 2,000
Federal Subsidized Loan	$ 3,500
Total Award	$ 42,500
On-Campus Direct Cost	$ 54,500
Total Financial Aid Award	$ 42,500
Year 1 Total Out-of-Pocket Cost	$ 12,000

You are eligible to earn up to $2,000 in work-study.

The closest estimate for attending College D's net price in year 1 would be **at least $17,500** and could go up significantly depending on the indirect costs.

- The cost of attendance is $54,500 (direct, excluding indirect costs)
- The total amount of gift aid is $37,000
- The actual net price for the first year is $17,500 plus an unknown amount in indirect costs

***

In summary, determining the net cost of attendance for each of these colleges' first year may be a bit complicated. Colleges B & D mixed grants and loans, and the calculated estimated costs included loans. College C did not list federal aid options. The parent or student should follow-up with College C to inquire about federal aid. College D did not provide the actual cost of attendance. Additionally, College B added the Parent PLUS Loan in the estimated cost section of the award.

The next section shows you the net price comparisons by college.

Comparing Colleges on Out-of-pocket Costs

Table 5 shows how the values provided through the sample FALs appear in the Spreadsheet. Once I added the FAL information to the Spreadsheet, the out-of-pocket costs were calculated automatically, and college cost comparisons were available instantly.

According to Table 5, College A has the lowest net price, $19,650. College D's net price may seem lower, but it may go up once the indirect costs are added to the calculations. Once the indirect costs are determined for College D, they should be added to the Spreadsheet. College C would be the third least expensive college on the list. Additionally, since College C is missing information on federal aid, the net cost may be higher. In other words, if a student is eligible for federal grants, once those grants are added to the calculations, the net price for College C would decrease.

It is always a good idea to add information from the FALs to the Spreadsheet. This process will help you identify missing information, such as the indirect costs for College C or federal aid for College D.

Once you determine that the FAL is incomplete, follow the steps described in Chapter 2 to find the missing information, especially related to the total cost of attendance, or follow-up with the college. Once you have all the information added to *the Spreadsheet*, you'll better understand the total cost of attendance and the out-of-pocket costs.

You may want to take a few minutes now and add your FALs' values to the Spreadsheet. Have you identified any missing information related to the total cost of attendance? How do your colleges compare in terms of out-of-pocket costs or net price?

Now that you have all the information in one place and know the net price for each college, the next chapter provides guidance on asking colleges for more aid.

Table 5: Net Price Comparison by College and Source of Aid

Cost of Attendance Total	College A	College B	College C	College D
Direct Costs				
Tuition and Fees	$ 15,500	$ 48,680	$ 28,800	(not provided)
Room and Board	$ 13,000	$ 15,300	$ 11,000	(not provided)
Total Direct Costs	$ 28,500	$ 63,980	$ 39,800	$ 54,500
Indirect Costs				
Estimated Books & Supplies	$ 1,350	$ 1,000	$ 850	(not provided)
Estimated Other Expenses	$ 3,700	$ 2,300	$ 2,700	(not provided)
Total Indirect Costs	$ 5,050	$ 3,300	$ 3,550	
Total Cost of Attendance (Direct + Indirect Costs)	**$ 33,550**	**$ 67,280**	**$ 43,350**	**$ 54,500+**
Gift Aid				
Pell Grant	$ 2,000	$ 2,000		$ 2,000
Federal FSEOG				
Total State Awards (Scholarships and Grants)	$ 5,900			
Total Institutional Awards (Scholarships and Grants)	$ 6,000	$ 28,500	$ 2,600	$ 35,000
Other Awards (Scholarships and Grants)				
Tuition Waiver			$ 6,000	
Total Gift Aid	**$ 13,900**	**$ 30,500**	**$ 8,600**	**$ 37,000**
Out-of-pocket Cost or Net Price for Year 1 (Total cost of attendance minus total gift aid)	**$ 19,650**	**$ 36,780**	**$ 34,750**	**$ 17,500+**
Loan Aid - Requires Repayment with Interest				
Federal Subsidized Stafford Loan	$ 3,500	$ 3,500		$ 3,500
Federal Unsubsidized Stafford Loan	$ 2,000	$ 2,000		$ 2,000
Federal Parent PLUS Loan		$ 29,280		
Total Loan Aid	$ 5,500	$ 34,780		$ 5,500
Earned Aid - Requires Working on Campus				
Federal Work-study	$ 2,000	$ 2,000		$ 2,000
Campus Employment				
Total Earned Aid	$ 2,000	$ 2,000		$ 2,000

CHAPTER 4: Ask for More Aid

By now, you should have a clear idea of how much each college will cost for the first year (net price) and how you can finance it (gift, loan, or earned aid). Now is the best time to reveal a couple of secrets: (1) yes, you can ask colleges for more assistance, and (2) financial aid officers have a certain level of discretion when putting together financial aid packages.

Financial aid officers may revise financial aid packets under certain circumstances, and these revisions may translate into more aid. To get considered for these revisions, you and your teen will need to appeal the financial aid packet.

There are two parts to the financial aid packet. The merit part and the need part. Merit refers to funds – typically scholarships – awarded based on academic achievements, such as high test scores or High School GPA. The need part refers to aid that is awarded based on demonstrated financial need. Financial aid officers can revise the merit or need or both sections of the offer.

As you will see next, each type of aid has a different process for appeal. Appealing the merit aid part requires information on academic achievements and sometimes other service activities or student attributes. Appealing the need aid part requires all kinds of income and expenses information and documentation.

The following section discusses how to go about asking for more aid or appealing each part of the financial aid letter.

Ask for More Merit Aid

Colleges may be willing to work with you and your teen to increase the merit aid under certain circumstances. But you'll have to be very specific when asking for more aid.

What could you get?

First, know that merit aid will typically come from the college-based funds (i.e., institutional aid). The reason for this is that the federal government does not award merit aid. The state governments have precise rules for awarding merit aid, so financial aid officers are unlikely to provide merit aid from these two pots of money. But as we discussed before, colleges often have this extra pot of money – typically help in their foundation – and financial aid (FA) officers know the eligibility guidelines and procedures for awarding these funds. In other words, if you make a persuasive case for additional merit aid, the financial aid officer may be able to tap into these funds to increase your award.

Now that we know that the source for more merit aid is the college and its funds, here are a few ways in which the college can provide your teen more aid:

- Additional scholarship funds – this is straight forward – the college increases the amount of the current gift aid or awards an additional scholarship
- Tuition waiver – the college decides to not charge the student for a certain number of credit hours per semester or per year
- Campus employment – the college offers the student the ability to work on campus and earn a paycheck
- A combination of the elements included above

As you may expect, private colleges tend to have more wiggle room with their institutional aid funds than public ones. But it is not uncommon to receive either one of these variations of merit aid from a public college.

Who should do it?

First, here's how things stand at the macro level. Each year tens of thousands of students apply to thousands of colleges. If your teen is like the average teen out there, they may have applied to at least six (6) schools. For example, during the last three admission cycles, many students applied to about 15-20 colleges. This may have been due to teens taking advantage of colleges' waiving application fees and the easy application features provided through the CommonApp or other college application software.

Second, on the college side, admissions and FA office staff have been working diligently on picking the students to accept and packaging them with financial aid. This process typically puts a tremendous amount of pressure on staff in both offices.

Third, there are three metrics to watch in the world of enrollment management: applied, admitted, and enrolled. Applied refers to the number of students that applied. Admitted refers to the number and percent of admitted students (also commonly referred to as selectivity). Finally, enrolled refers to the students who accepted the offer of admission and then enrolled at the college.

It is important to know that even though the number of applicants and admitted students may be large, colleges may encounter difficulties getting enough students to enroll. A significant portion of colleges tends to run into this problem when building their incoming class. Of course, this will not be the case at the Harvards and Stanfords of the world, but the reality is that these colleges represent only a small fraction of all colleges and students.

Consequently, the sooner a college builds its incoming class, the better. Therefore, the sooner you appeal, the more likely there will be funds available to help you.
With this in mind, let's explore the process of appealing merit aid.

Once your teen decides on which college they would really like to attend, start thinking about making an argument as to why your teen's request for more merit aid should be granted. Pull out your Spreadsheet and begin drafting an email to the FA office to explain the amount of assistance you are looking for to make you deposit with the college.

Before getting too excited, know that not all colleges grant these appeals, but the fact is that you have nothing to lose, as existing awards will not disappear from the financial aid letter just because you asked for more. It's worth a try.

How to go about it?

Now that we know what could be gained let's see what evidence you could provide to strengthen your request for more aid. Start drafting the appeal email, and as we are going through the rest of the chapter, include as much supporting data and arguments into that email as possible as to why your teen deserves more aid.

1. High School GPA
Examine your teen's high school GPA (HSGPA) vs. the average HSGPA for a past incoming class to understand where you stand.

If you haven't done so already, check out the average GPA for a prior incoming class at the college you are interested in attending. See if your teen's HS GPA is higher and by how much.

To find out the HSGPA for a previous incoming class, go to the Princeton Review website and look up the college. In the Admissions section, you may find the average HSGPA and maybe even an HSGPA breakdown. Colleges report HSGPA information to external entities, such as Princeton Review through the Common Dataset. Reporting this information is not required, and some schools may choose not to do it. Additionally, some colleges don't fill out the Common Data Set every year. In other words, you may not be able to find the HSGPA for all colleges or the most recent prior year.

If you find the college's HSGPA and your teen's HSGPA is higher than the average and in the top intervals of the breakdown, then use this information for the merit aid request.

2. *Test Scores*
Many colleges went test-optional starting with fall 2021, and many more joined them over time. But test-optional is not test-blind, and those scores may still carry some weight, especially if your teen did well on them.

Doing well on these tests is a relative term. Results are not weighed versus how well all the other test-takers did, but versus how well the students that enrolled at the college during the prior year did. As you see now, doing well varies by who is being compared to your teen. Your teen should not look at their scores and percentile and despair; instead, they should look at the scores of the students that enrolled at that specific college in the past. Here's how to get to test scores of students that enrolled at the college during the last fall.

We are going back to the College Navigator, our "go-to" source for accurate and up to date information, https://nces.ed.gov/collegenavigator/, and search for your college. In the new window, open the "Admissions" section and look at the 25th to 75th percentile score range. Figure 1 includes an example of 25th to 75th percentile scores for students that enrolled in a specific college during Fall 2020.

Now compare and contrast your teen's scores with the 25th-75th percentile range. If they scored somewhat close to, at, or above the 75th percentile, then include this information in the email you are drafting when requesting more aid.

Figure 1: Sample Admissions information in College Navigator

TEST SCORES: FALL 2019 (ENROLLED FIRST-TIME STUDENTS)

STUDENTS SUBMITTING SCORES	NUMBER	PERCENT
SAT	1,201	88%
ACT	704	52%

TEST SCORES	25TH PERCENTILE*	75TH PERCENTILE**
SAT Evidence-Based Reading and Writing	530	590
SAT Math	500	570
ACT Composite	19	23
ACT English	18	23
ACT Math	17	23

NOTES:
* 25% of students scored at or below
** 25% of students scored above

- Data apply to first-time degree/certificate-seeking students
- Institutions are asked to report test scores only if they are required for admission

3. Average Financial Aid

Another element that you may want to consider as you are drafting the email asking for more financial aid is the average net price. College Navigator has this information – so go back to the website and open the "Net Price" section and check out the average value for the college or by income quintile. Again, the net price is the amount of money that students and parents need to pay for the first year of college. Figure 2 includes the average net price by income quintile.

There are two things to keep in mind in terms of Net Price from College Navigator. First, the Net Price values are averages, so some families/students pay more while others pay less. Second, the Average Net Price is calculated only for private colleges and in-state students attending in-state public colleges. Therefore, do not use the Average Net Price when looking at out-of-state public colleges, as this value is not available.

If your teen plans to attend an in-state public college or a private college, use the Average Net Price information as provided in College Navigator to get an idea of how much more aid you may want to ask for.

Figure 2: Sample Net Price information in College Navigator

⊖ NET PRICE

AVERAGE NET PRICE FOR FULL-TIME BEGINNING STUDENTS

Full-time beginning undergraduate students who were awarded grant or scholarship aid from federal, state or local governments, or the Institution.

	2016-2017	2017-2018	2018-2019
Average net price	$41,536	$44,063	$45,356

Full-time beginning undergraduate students who were awarded Title IV aid by income.

AVERAGE NET PRICE BY INCOME	2016-2017	2017-2018	2018-2019
$0 – $30,000	$32,462	$31,389	$34,276
$30,001 – $48,000	$30,719	$31,311	$33,304
$48,001 – $75,000	$32,784	$34,995	$34,599
$75,001 – $110,000	$35,789	$38,236	$39,241
$110,001 and more	$41,287	$42,725	$42,586

- Average net price is generated by subtracting the average amount of federal, state/local government, or institutional grant or scholarship aid from the total cost of attendance. Total cost of attendance is the sum of published tuition and required fees, books and supplies, and the weighted average for room and board and other expenses.
- Beginning students are those who are entering postsecondary education for the first time.
- Title IV aid to students includes grant aid, work study aid, and loan aid. These include: Federal Pell Grant, Federal Supplemental Educational Opportunity Grant (FSEOG), Academic Competitiveness Grant (ACG), National Science and Mathematics Access to Retain Talent Grant (National SMART Grant), Teacher Education Assistance for College and Higher Education (TEACH) Grant, Federal Work-Study, Federal Perkins Loan, Subsidized Direct or FFEL Stafford Loan, and Unsubsidized Direct or FFEL Stafford Loan. For those Title IV recipients, net price is reported by income category and includes students who received federal aid even if none of that aid was provided in the form of grants. While Title IV status defines the cohort of student for which the data are reported, the definition of net price remains the same – total cost of attendance minus grant aid.

Compare and contrast your net price or out-of-pocket cost with the values included in College Navigator for the college you are interested in. If your Net Price is significantly higher, you may want to add that fact in the draft email requesting more merit aid to lower your net price.

4. *Look at Other Financial Aid Packages from Similar Colleges*

Open the Spreadsheet and look at the net price from each college that accepted your teen. Examine the net price and merit aid from all the colleges similar to the one you'd like to ask for more aid. If another similar college awarded more merit aid, use that information to argue for more financial assistance in the appeal email.

5. *Praise & Commitment*

A little bit of praise goes a long way. First, try to explain in the email why your teen is dead set on the college and the program. Showering the college with a little bit of praise will help you make your case and smoothen the way to more aid.

Second, have a very clear idea of the amount that would make your teen commit to the college and ask for it in the appeal email.

Third, be ready to commit. Once the college honors your request, it expects commitment. Don't go through all this trouble if you and your teen are not prepared to commit to the college.

***

Overall, there are three things to keep in mind here. First, there are no guarantees that your appeal will be granted, but it does not hurt to ask. Second, do your homework. Have a very clear idea about the amount that will make you and your teen commit to the college and send in the deposit. Third, and this cannot be emphasized enough, if you do get the additional merit aid funds, request that these funds are not only for the first year but also renewable for the duration of the studies. The next chapter, "What happens to aid in subsequent years," discusses grants and scholarship renewability and what factors to pay attention to as you are evaluating financial aid packages.

Now that we have a clear idea about how to appeal the merit aid part, let's discuss how to appeal the need aid part of the financial aid packet.

Ask for More Need Aid

Need aid refers to aid that is awarded in response to demonstrated financial need. While the only source of additional merit aid was the college, the sources of need aid are more diverse, including the federal government and potentially the state government and the college. I say potentially for state government and college, because some states and colleges may award need aid, while others may not. It all depends on the state and the college. The thing to keep in mind here is that financial aid officers have a certain degree of discretion (called professional judgment) to revise the need aid part of the packet.

What could you get?

Now that we know the potential sources of need aid, here are a few ways in which the college can provide your teen with more need aid:

- Becoming eligible for Pell Grant or a higher amount of Pell Grant.
- Becoming eligible for subsidized loans. The federal government pays the interest on subsidized loans for as long as the student is in school. Subsidized loans are the best type of loans available for financing an education.
- Becoming eligible for federal work-study.
- Becoming eligible for state grants. Some states offer only need aid, while others provide only merit aid. There are, however, some states that offer both need and merit aid. If your state provides need aid, your teen may become eligible for it.

- Becoming eligible for need-based grants from college funds or institutional aid. Some colleges offer these grants, and your teen may qualify for them.

Even if your teen already received need-based aid, but the family finances deteriorated, it might be worth the effort to appeal the need based aid part of the FAL.

Who should do it?

Most of the need-based aid included in the FAL is awarded based on information from the FAFSA, sometimes the CSS profile, and other state-specific applications. Many financial aid offices across the country build financial aid packages to the best of their knowledge and within the guidelines specified by the federal and state governments and the college's goals.

The issue is the timing of submitting tax information to colleges. All of these applications, especially the FAFSA, use income from two years ago. A lot of things can happen to family finances in two years.

Even so, the college costs and demand for education didn't decrease. On the one hand, some colleges may have increased their costs months before the crisis was even on the horizon. On the other hand, if jobs are scarce, pay tends to be low; if salaries are small, going to college would not prevent people from earning money. Hence, the demand for education did not decrease.

Times of economic contraction might present students and parents with an opportunity to make a case for a revised financial aid packet if income changed significantly because of a job loss or furlough. Students and families who can provide documentation and demonstrate decreases in family income (for dependent students) or individual income (for independent students) may be able to secure more need-based aid.

Using their "professional judgment," financial aid officers can re-evaluate and update the financial aid packet under certain circumstances on a case-by-case basis. You will be required to provide lots of documentation substantiating the income loss, but know that it is possible.

Another scenario where professional judgment comes in handy is when a family is experiencing a one-time spike in finances, such as selling a home or other assets. If the year with high income has to be used for FAFSA, that information will impact how much need-based aid your teen will receive. A divorce or increases in medical bills may also warrant a request for professional judgment.

In summary, during challenging economic times, professional judgment can come in handy and help students and families pay for college. The FALs for fall 2021 were based on 2019 tax information, and for fall 2022 were based on 2020 tax information. Suppose your teen will start college during the fall of 2023 or spring of 2024, and your finances have decreased significantly since tax year 2021. In that case, you may want to appeal the need-based aid part of the FAL and may benefit from financial aid officers' professional judgment.

How to go about it?

While FA officers do have discretion when creating the packet, they'll need lots of documentation to justify changes to need aid or the overall financial aid packet. Colleges—like almost anything out there—are bureaucracies. They get audited by various entities regularly. Because of this, documentation is vital for informing the decision-making process involved in professional judgment.

To start the process, draft an email explaining how your financial situation has changed and provide as much documentation as possible. If one of the parents lost a job, was furloughed, or medical expenses increased, attach a copy of each of these documents to the email requesting revisions to need-based aid. Financial aid officers may also follow-up with you and request additional documents.

***

One word of advice: if you are planning on using this process, be kind. Financial aid officers work very hard to make good for the student and the college. Be kind and considerate with them.

Remember that you can appeal each part of the financial aid packet (merit or need). Depending on your circumstances, you and your teen may want to appeal only one part or both.

You may want to wait until you have all the financial aid letters from all the colleges that accepted your teen before starting the appeal process. Having this information will help you get an idea of how much aid your teen secured in merit aid and how much aid would make your teen commit to their dream college. If you plan to appeal the need aid part of the FAL, it would be best to complete both the merit and need aid parts in one step, rather than appealing the merit first and need aid second. In the meantime, start working on making an argument for more aid and collect documentation to support the appeal.

Independent of which part you plan to appeal, put everything in one email and make sure you provide as much justification and as many supporting documents as you can. Have a clear idea of how much aid you are looking for, and be thorough in justifying the appeal. Start the process as soon as you can do so in a prepared way. Be kind and considerate, as the process may take a little bit of time.

CHAPTER 5: What Happens to Aid after the First Year

The calculations included previously refer only to the first year of college; net price during the second and subsequent years may change. There are various reasons why the costs may change as students' progress through college. Here is a starter list of potential changes that can impact eligibility for aid in subsequent years. Keep them in mind as you are evaluating financial aid packages.

I. Federal Funds (Grants & Loans)
Changes in Income. Changes in income or finances are very common, such as a parent finding a job after a period of unemployment, receiving a raise at their current job, or finding a better paying job. Any changes to family

finances can lead to changes in the Pell Grant amount, especially for dependent students.

Conversely, a parent losing their job may lead to changes in federal funds. Under this scenario, students may become eligible for new or additional federal funds in grants and loans.

Satisfactory Academic Progress (SAP) Requirements. The Pell Grant has an SAP requirement. Students who receive a Pell Grant need to meet specific SAP standards to retain eligibility for the grant. These SAP requirements may refer to maintaining a certain GPA, but SAPs are specific to every college. Find out what the SAP requirements are for your college and save a copy for your records.

Filing FAFSA Every Year. Students need to file their FAFSA every year. Failing to do so will prevent them from gaining or retaining federal funds eligibility (grants, loans, and work-study).

II. State and Institutional Awards (Grants and Scholarships)

Changes in Award Amounts. Changes to state funds may occur over time. Because state funds are allocated to students directly from a state's budget, some states may revise the amounts associated with grants and scholarships from time to time.

Additionally, institutional award amounts may also change over time. Institutional aid refers to awards (grants and scholarships) that are funded by the institution. Every once in a while, colleges revise their policies, rules, and regulations. Revisions may lead to changes in criteria for awarding institutional aid and the dollar amounts associated with these awards. Changes in these awards tend to be rare, but they are not uncommon.

First-Year Awards. State or institutional awards may be available only for the first year, and hence non-renewable. Consequently, students and parents will need to make up the costs during the subsequent years. An excellent example of such awards are scholarships provided for visiting the campus. These scholarships range from a few hundred to a couple of thousand dollars and are non-renewable for the second year.

Changes in GPA. Some awards, especially the merit-based ones, require students to maintain a certain GPA for the award to be renewed.

It is quite common for students to experience a decrease in GPA during freshman year. It may be due to various reasons, such as juggling work, classes, study time, socializing, and sometimes family demands, such as caring for other family members. Another common reason for GPA decreases is the difference between high school and college standards. College standards tend to be more stringent, and students may need a little bit of time to adjust to them. A student who used to get A's in high school may start getting other grades in college, thus influencing their GPA. A Berkeley study found that "mean [college] GPAs plummeted well below what students have become accustomed to earning in high school," noting that the mean high school GPA of 3.52 decreased to 2.97 after the first year of college (Geiser and Santelices, 2007, p. 17). These changes can place students in danger of losing significant amounts of institutional aid. Students who are aware of these GPA requirements and study hard should be fine.

Conversely, increases in a student's GPA may help them gain eligibility for additional gift aid.

Students need to pay attention to the GPA or SAP requirements because failing to meet them may lead to award loss. Awards may have grace periods where a student may receive an additional term to bring up their GPA, but it all depends on the college and its rules.

III. Tuition Waivers

Tuition waivers may change over time. Similar to grants and scholarships, learn the renewability criteria for these tuition waivers so that your teen can hang on to them for as long as possible. A student that loses the tuition waiver will need to figure out a way to make up the difference.

Overall, students may gain or lose eligibility for gift aid as they progress throughout their college years. Some may gain eligibility for additional gift aid, while others lose it. It is quite common for students to lose eligibility for gift aid. When that happens, the net price or out-of-pocket cost goes up, and the student needs to find a way to cover it. It is important to keep these things in mind as you are evaluating financial aid packages.

IV. Cost of Attendance Increases

Another area to pay attention to is the cost of attendance. Whether it be higher tuition, fees, or more expensive room and board, increases in the cost of attendance are quite common.

There are many reasons for these increases. For example, recessions tend to prompt increases in the cost of attendance for colleges heavily reliant on state support. During recessions, states tend to decrease colleges' support; therefore, some colleges may increase their tuition and fees to bridge the gap. Additionally, colleges may increase their cost of attendance to keep up with the cost of living and remain competitive.

All in all, increases in attendance costs are not uncommon, and financial aid awards tend not to account for them. When these increases occur, students must be prepared to cover them.

It is important to emphasize that the dollar amounts associated with awards may change over time. Consequently, the financial aid packet may look different as a student progresses through their college years.

CHAPTER 6: Select the Best College for You

Now you have all the data in front of you. By now, you know what each element of the financial aid letter means, the out-of-pocket cost for each college, how to ask for more aid, and how aid can change in subsequent years. At this point, you may face one of the following scenarios:

- The college that your teen would like to attend is a bit more expensive than expected.
- There are a couple of colleges that your teen would love to attend but cannot decide on one.
- You'd like to learn more information on key metrics for the college or post-graduation outcomes.

If you or your teen find yourselves in any of these scenarios, help is on the way!

Many high school counselors will tell you that the college selection decision should consider academic and financial fit, accurate data, and practicality. Some teens may have their hearts set on one specific college; others may want to compare costs and find the best balance between what they want and what is feasible. If you and your teen have difficulty deciding on one college, then looking up actual stats can help you compare them objectively and inform your college selection decision.

Here are a few stats that can provide you with valuable information and help you decide:

- Graduation rates
- Salary after graduation
- How much debt is too much
- Experiential learning

Graduation Rates

One important statistic to consider is the graduation rate, which has had its share of controversy. First off, it's hard to understand; second, it excludes certain groups of students. Here's what you need to know about the graduation rate.

Graduation rates track the percentage of students who graduate with bachelor's degrees from the same college four or six years later.

First off, the graduation rates only refer to students who enrolled in college full-time immediately after graduating from high school. If your teen follows the same path, then graduation rates can be meaningful to you and provide a good indication of how much time your teen may need to complete their college degree.

The standard for measuring college graduation rates is set at 6 years, not 4. If you used any college guides that provided a graduation rate without specifying whether it was for 4 years or 6, then it referred to the 6-year graduation rate by default.

The issue is that each additional college term past the 4-year mark can become costly for the student and their family. One study found that each extra year spent in college after the 4-year mark can cost students "an additional $469 per month in loan payments." So what may have been a $500 loan payment would nearly double to $969 per month. In addition to this, students delaying graduation may incur extra costs, commonly referred to as opportunity costs. Opportunity costs refer to lost wages for the years they were still in school, after the 4-year mark. These costs "will generally be even" higher than the other expenses discussed before. Therefore, parents and students should be aware of the 4- and 6-year graduation rates when selecting a college.[22]

Here is how to find the graduation rates:
- Go to College Navigator and search for the name of the college
- Go to the "Retention and Graduation Rates" section
- Scroll down to the "Bachelor's Degree Graduation Rates" section to find the most recent stats available for 4-year graduation rates

I've included an example in Figure 3 that shows how the graduation rate looks like in College Navigator. Here's how to read it: of all the new students who enrolled in college full-time during the fall of 2013 (immediately after high school graduation), 68% graduated in 4 years, and 83% graduated in 6 years.

Figure 3: Graduation Rates

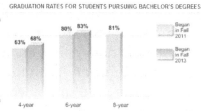

Percentage of Full-time, First-time Students Who Graduated in the Specified Amount of Time and Began in Fall 2011 or Fall 2013

The data included in Figure 3 is from a college with above-average graduation rates. The average 4-year graduation rate is approximately 41%, and the 6-year graduation rate is around 60% at the national level.[23,24] Put differently, about four in ten students who enroll full-time immediately after graduating high school graduate from the same college in 4 years, and two additional students, or six in ten, do so in 6 years. Obviously, the higher the graduation rate, the better.

Salary After Graduation
Two other new data points that could inform your teen's college decision are *salary after graduation* and *median salary by field of study*. The College Scorecard https://collegescorecard.ed.gov, maintained by the US Department of Education (USDOE), provides this information in a way that is easy to read and understand.

While the website includes the following disclaimer: the USDOE "cannot fully confirm the completeness of these reported data for this school," these new data points are a significant step in the right direction. With time, this data will become more and more complete and highly informative. In the meantime, know that this information is available and can shed some light on potential earnings after graduation.

How Much Debt Is Too Much?
The salary data provided by the College Scorecard can also be used as a good indicator as to how much debt is reasonable for students to take on to finance their college studies.

The rule of thumb is that the total amount of debt a student should take on for the entire college duration should not exceed their first-year salary. For example, suppose a student pursues a bachelor's degree in accounting, and the average salary after graduation is $52,000. In that case, the student should not borrow more than $52,000 for the entire duration of their undergraduate studies for that degree.

While salary data is approximate, it does provide a reasonably good estimate of how much debt may be too much.

Experiential Learning
Another good indicator for deciding which college to deposit with is the experiential learning requirement.

Experiential learning has become popular in the past few years. It developed in direct response to college engagement research and job market demands. In an effort to help students experience a seamless transition between the world of college and the world of work, colleges structured internships, co-ops, research courses, study abroad programs, and leadership experiences. They put them all under the experiential learning umbrella. While internships, co-ops, etc., have been available to some extent in the past, the advent of experiential learning structured these options. It ensured that each student could and at some colleges must pursue at least one of these opportunities before graduating from college. The best way to learn about whether a college has an experiential learning requirement is its website.

All in all, these indicators may complement the data that you already have on colleges and can help inform the college selection decision-making process.

Conclusion

Phew—you are almost done! You've been through a roller coaster of stress, anxiety, endless to-do lists, and activities, but the prize is in sight. The conclusion of this process might be bittersweet as it might involve you dropping off your teen at a college miles away from home this upcoming fall. This is always a hard thing to do.

Now is the time for your teen to spread their wings and soar as they prepare for their future. You did your absolute best, and I am sure they will make you proud as they pursue their dreams and make our world a better place.

Before you leave, I want to ask for a tiny favor. If you got anything out of this book, had any sort of "aha" moment, or felt that the information provided here made a difference for you or your teen, please consider giving a copy of it to someone else, leaving a review, making a video, commenting about it on social media, or anything really—anything to show that you found it beneficial and that it may help others navigate the college admissions maze successfully. It would mean a lot to me.

Now send in that deposit and start dorm shopping! The future is bright!

Acknowledgements

It takes a village to write a book and this one is no exception.

I am especially grateful to my husband Adrian for all his support and encouragements during this time. His kind nudges and encouragements helped me put one foot in front of another when the research, writing, and publishing process became overwhelming. He was there to discuss with me each section of the book, its flow, and logic.

Much appreciation for and gratefulness for three Ladies in my life. I am extremely grateful to my dear mentor Dr. Gita Pitter for our extensive conversations on complex concepts and college and university expectations. Grateful for our walks and extremely informative conversations on issues that parents and students face regarding college selection, admission, and finances.

My sincere thanks to my dear friend Dr. Lauren Haddad-Freidman for all her support throughout this process. Her reading, editing, and questioning have helped polish this book.

A heartfelt thank you to my dear friend Dr. Maya Ackerman for her unconditional friendship and support over the years. For reading and providing feedback on the book and graciously agreeing to write the foreword to it. I am deeply grateful for our friendship and collaboration.

A sincere thank you to everyone who read and provided feedback for the book that helped polish it – Lianna Barbu, Richard Stevens, Adina Pernes, and Bianca Lupsha. Also, many thanks to Yami Rial for graciously addressing my financial aid questions.

Many thanks to Lupsha Research, LLC., lupsha.com for providing the IT backbone for www.CollegeTalk.us.

About the Author

Diana Barbu, Ph.D., or "Dr. Diana," is committed to helping students graduate in four years with the least amount of debt. Dr. Diana served as the Associate Vice-Provost of Institutional Research and Effectiveness at St. Thomas University, as the Director of Research and Data Analytics at Miami Dade College, and as the Director of Academic Programs at The State University System of Florida – Board of Governors. She holds a Ph.D. in Higher Education from Florida State University, a Master in Communication from Rutgers University, and a Bachelor of Science in Computer Science and Mathematics.

Using her senior leadership experience at public and private colleges, Dr. Diana points parents and students to accurate, actionable information to help with the college admission decision. She offers strategies and tools to help parents and students find the best academic and financial fit for their unique needs.

Scan the code below to access the latest resources on www.CollegeTalk.us

Appendix A: The Cost Comparison Spreadsheet

Cost of attendance Total		College A	College Name
Direct Costs			
Tuition and Fees	$	15,500	
Room and Board	$	13,000	
Total Direct Costs	$	**28,500**	Total of Direct Costs
Indirect Costs			
Estimated Books & Supplies	$	1,350	
Estimated Other Expenses	$	3,700	
Total Indirect Costs	$	**5,050**	Total of Indirect Costs
Total Cost of Attendance	**$**	**33,550**	Direct + Indirect Costs
Gift Aid			
Pell Grant	$	2,000	
Federal FSEOG			
Total State Scholarships and Grants	$	5,900	
Total Institutional Scholarships and Grants	$	6,000	
Other Scholarships and Grants			
Tuition Waiver			
Total Gift Aid	**$**	**13,900**	Total Gift Aid
Net Cost or Out-of-Pocket Costs for Year 1	**$**	**19,650**	Total Cost of Attendance - Total Gift Aid
Loan Aid - Requires Repayment with Interest			
Federal Subsidized Stafford Loan	$	3,500	
Federal Unsubsidized Stafford Loan	$	2,000	
Federal Parent PLUS Loan			
Total Loan aid	**$**	**5,500**	Total Loan Aid
Earned Aid - Requires Working			
Federal Work Study	$	2,000	
Campus Employment			
Total Earned aid	**$**	**2,000**	Total Earned Aid

Scan the code below to download the Excel version of this document.

List of Abbreviations

SAI/EFC – the Student Aid Index (SAI) replaces the Expected Family Contribution (EFC) effective October 1, 2022. The SAI is "an index that reflects an evaluation of a student's approximate financial resources to contribute toward the student's postsecondary education for the academic year." Starting October 1, 2022 the SAI replaces the EFC. The EFC was "a measure of how much the student and his or her family can be expected to contribute to the cost of the student's education for the year."[25]

FAFSA - the Free Application for Federal Student Aid

FAL – Financial Aid Letter

FSEOG - Federal Supplemental Educational Opportunity Grant

SAP – Satisfactory Academic Progress

Sticker Price – the total cost of attendance

Net Price or Out-of-pocket Cost – how much money a student will have to pay out-of-pocket to attend college for one year.

References

Geiser, S., & Santelices, M. V. (2007). Validity of High-School Grades in Predicting Student Success beyond the Freshman Year: High-School Record vs. Standardized Tests as Indicators of Four-Year College Outcomes. Research & Occasional Paper Series: CSHE. 6.07. *Center for studies in higher education*.

Goldrick-Rab, S. (2016). *Paying the price: College costs, financial aid, and the betrayal of the American dream*. University of Chicago Press.

Notes

[1]https://www.princetonreview.com/cms-
content/TPR_College_Hopes_Worries_2020_Report.pdf
[2]https://www.forbes.com/sites/zackfriedman/2020/02
/03/student-loan-debt-statistics/#4350806e281f
[3]https://www.kansascityfed.org/publications/ten/artic
les/2019/summer2019/after-soaring-for-years-college-
tuition-has-slowed-significantly
[4]https://masfaa.org/wp-
content/uploads/2021/06/Consolidated-
Appropriations-Act-2021.pdf
[5]https://citeseerx.ist.psu.edu/viewdoc/download?doi=
10.1.1.188.6805&rep=rep1&type=pdf
[6]https://studentaid.gov/help-
center/answers/article/what-does-net-price-mean-for-
college-costs
[7]https://www.forbes.com/sites/zackfriedman/2020/02
/03/student-loan-debt-statistics/#4350806e281f
[8]https://www.forbes.com/sites/zackfriedman/2020/02
/03/student-loan-debt-statistics/#4350806e281f
[9]https://www.cnbc.com/2019/01/03/car-payments-
and-loans-jump-amid-surging-demand-for-cars-
suvs.html
[10]https://www.experian.com/blogs/ask-
experian/what-is-the-average-car-payment/

[11]https://ticas.org/wp-content/uploads/2019/09/classof2018.pdf
[12]https://www.federalreserve.gov/publications/2019-economic-well-being-of-us-households-in-2018-student-loans-and-other-education-debt.htm
[13]https://studentaid.gov/understand-aid/types/loans/interest-rates
[14]https://www.newamerica.org/education-policy/policy-papers/decoding-cost-college/
[15] https://studentaid.gov/understand-aid/types/loans/plus/parent#what-is-the-current-interest-rate
[16]https://ticas.org/wp-content/uploads/2019/09/classof2018.pdf
[17]https://studentaid.gov/complete-aid-process/accept-aid
[18]https://ticas.org/wp-content/uploads/2019/09/classof2018.pdf
[19]https://www.newamerica.org/education-policy/policy-papers/decoding-cost-college/
[20]https://ticas.org/files/pub_files/cost_in_translation.pdf
[21]https://www2.ed.gov/policy/highered/guid/aid-offer/index.html
[22]https://www.brookings.edu/research/time-to-graduation-too-often-overlooked/
[23]https://nces.ed.gov/programs/coe/indicator_ctr.asp
[24]https://nces.ed.gov/programs/raceindicators/indicator_red.asp
[25]https://masfaa.org/wp-content/uploads/2021/06/Consolidated-Appropriations-Act-2021.pdf

Made in the USA
Las Vegas, NV
13 February 2024

85734979R00073